TANGLED THREADS

by

Margo Von Strohuber

BLUE LIGHT PRESS ◆ 1ST WORLD PUBLISHING

1ST WORLD
PUBLISHING

SAN FRANCISCO ◆ FAIRFIELD ◆ DELHI

WINNER OF THE 2016 BLUE LIGHT POETRY PRIZE

TANGLED THREADS

Copyright ©2017 by Margo Von Strohuber

1ST WORLD LIBRARY
PO Box 2211
Fairfield, IA 52556
www.1stworldpublishing.com

BLUE LIGHT PRESS
www.bluelightpress.com
Email: bluelightpress@aol.com

BOOK & COVER DESIGN
Melanie Gendron
www.melaniegendron.com

COVER ART
Melanie Gendron

FIRST EDITION

ISBN: 978-1-4218-3779-6

Praise for *Tangled Threads*

"The tangible power of love so seductively expressed. The compelling verses made a beeline to my heart."

—Diane Denbaum, Author of
Madly in Love Forever.

"I love them. . . they are direct. . . reach right out and pull you in, accessible, easy to follow and understand, yet with surprising images and unpredictable word play. . . dense with meaning they delight the mind, and also touch the heart, make vulnerability safe. I had several aha experiences reading these poems, recognizing my own heretofore unnamed, unexpressed moments. Finally, they roll off the tongue, rich with alliteration and internal rhyme. They beg to be read aloud, even if no one else is there to hear."

—Carol Olicker

"I've been following Margo Von Strohuber's writing for many years, and the poems in *Tangled Threads* are her best. What I most admire in these poems is the raw passion and fierce minimalism. Every line is transparent to the emotions. Every poem in this book is a jewel."

—Diane Frank, Author of *Canon for Bears and Ponderosa Pines*

"Margo von Strohuber's lively poems sing with wit, intelligence, and passion. With a poet's finely tuned ear and wicked sharp intelligence these poems consume the reader in the true art of poetry. They do the hard work of speaking the truths that lie beyond polite assumptions. They are brave, smart, full of heart and wisdom with a smidge of laugh out loud chuckles to boot. Do not miss these poems. Among the best I've read in ages."

—Meg Hill Fitz-Randolph

FORWARD

Under the critical eye I'm a fool for the foibles and passions of the human heart—for that we are all forgiven—but in truth, a tale of wandering love interrupted is more fantasy than the mundane homebody I am. I find ease in the love of my longtime companion, Judy, together on the slow track of aging gracefully, grateful for friends and family. If left in question, not knowing what really happened or the magic of poetry, choose poetry.

CONTENTS

Tangled threads
of tired, straight-laced
silent dreams,
uneven seams,
nothing
to knit or knot
or cobble up.
Quiet sparks that
smolder in the dark
make language luminous,
less discrete.
But quick, bright,
orange dawn
finds my finger
frozen on delete.

Do you want to rescue me
as I do you?
What a funny pair of odd birds
dropping feathers to furnish a perilous perch.
I agree I want to cozy up, lean in,
serene in this warmth.
Down does what desperate time's whore
can't wait for:
warms without intent,
accepts the easy payment of yes,
plans a party for beaky friends,
pontificates a plan to repent.

I am not strong
nor long on purity.
Wrong in all the ways that count.
If song is what you want,
then sing your highest notes
to wind and water;
finned or winged ones
will resound in kind.
I bless your life and hope
you'll never leave me
far behind.

I feel so seldom.
Mostly, I am numb,
would suck my thumb
but wine does such a better job
of quelling storms that rage inside
I can't allow my body to
let prurience decide me.
I wish I could escape and let
intellect discover
raw emotion,
become
the one
I wish I were.

I know what you need
and what you need is not me,
even as I would make you feel
Oh! and me too.
You deserve a better love
a sober, younger ahhh...
and even though I could
it would not be good for you.
Please accept a part of my damaged heart
It will strengthen yours
and jump start
an ardor stronger than my lust.
I am just
so sad.

Here is what I want to say:
Let's fuck,
but I know that we can't.
I am so smitten, and you
are probably torn in two.
This magnetic pull
which I wouldn't deny
even if I could
would end with flesh finding fingers
pressure applied, sigh!
Oh my darling, I lied when I said I had any control
over the outcome.

Hands do what the heart can't handle,
(being hidden, good for feeling but not much else)
Hands wipe tears and dry dishes,
greet friends and make love,
cook dinner, fold laundry
paint pictures, play songs.
Busy are hands 'til they finally rest
crossed on a chest,
atop their silent partner, the heart,
quiet at last.

I have no right to say this
but of course I will.
I want to stroke your hair
spoon your body with mine
make the pain recede
if only for a time.
Hands can foster miracles
a kiss will make sublime.

Should I up the ante?
The written word enchants me.
It allows for time, interpretation and release
and a fond, sweet spreading of desire.
Maybe it's the same composing
music while reposing in the moment
I know enough to know that what you do
is far beyond my means
and I really do admire you.

The muse doesn't stick around
She comes to tease and titillate
(I like that word)
She dumps on me a mess of words
I find I have to unscramble,
like a jigsaw puzzle
or a dog in a muzzle
wanting out.

This sweet solitary ache at 4 a.m.
leads to you.
My body vibrates, mind expands.
I am liquid, spreading layer
of erotic love
like honey on toast.
I cover you with my
warm mouth.
No delight too taboo.
I want all of you
from skin into soul,
hands that stroke, excite,
Igniting ecstasy.
Without barriers, our bodies
can become one.

In my fantasy,
I will make your skin sing,
stroke one-fingered
along the length of you
where body meets sheet
two-fingered, inside thighs
pausing,
pretending not to know
your pain.
Exquisite, slow
until you whimper, plead
with hot breath
and arched back,
Oh, so close
to voiceless victory.

There will be love!
Even though shackled to humdrum chores,
love steals in the door,
leaps from the lamp
crawls out of the floor
ambushes me in the midst
of folding sheets and towels
and scowls a delicious sigh.
Oh, and I try to squash it down
kick it to the back porch to freeze,
but love "keeps coming back"
as they say in AA.
It will do as it pleases
ravishing my good intentions
making jello of my limbs.
Singing hymns will not banish this joy,
not pleading, nor prayer.
I am love's slave
with you in its lair.

Two broken souls unite
find flint in the dark,
set spark to glow,
fight for freedom
and the time to grow
in green pastures.
Celebrate love in the light,
reach heights unknown,
rejoice in passion sown
in fertile soil.
Blaze tall along towering peaks
take our place in the
forest primeval.

Things I love about you:
The gentle timbre of your voice excites my soul.
Your hands...watching your genes surface in gestures,
imagining those hands on my body,
the size and shape of you, your eyes, your hair, your lips
loving the potential of you and me making music and art (and food!)
That you know I am not finished but still a work in progress.
How can I keep this joy to myself
when I long to share it with anyone who will listen?
The dead giveaway of my silly grin when I talk about you,
the fool I know I am and don't really care.
My desire for your unbounded optimism,
the pure joy of your spirit
the kiss of your eyes as they meet mine.

Stunned, my heart
flamed high,
I felt fine
my eyes' arms
holding all of you
tenderly, gingerly
wanting to kiss your voice
into silence,
lead our love
to the Himalayas
ready to farm
rice paddies
on terraced plots of green
like emeralds,
row upon row of lovely eyes
staring skyward
kissing God
who will bless us
in return.

A life lived remembers all the flesh felt,
stroked soft or bounced along the margins of
farm-fed skin folds, over moles and into star-shaped scars.
We frame our question to recall an answer:
Will you be the last lover to know me?
Will your hands see me into heaven?
Or hell? What about the 72 virgins
promised Muslim men. . . is it too late to convert
if being lesbian leads to the same result?
Or not! Good God, who would want
that many wanton women screeching along
the alliterative edge of knife-sharp night?
A frightening thought. I'll settle for you,
your kiss and scent and silver hair
and all the unknown habits I will find and cherish
along the path into our deeper wooded years.

This drum beat sounding slow
and steady
and enduring
at the bottom of my brain
The place where I don't think or conjure
rules or knowledge or hope. . .
This constant is you,
amorphous but forcibly
known.
You are with me through the days
and nights, as familiar as my name
I wear you like a cloak I cannot see,
You cover me and I know you
and feel your warmth,
as real as the sun
on my body
which longs to merge with yours.

Dreaming hands bunch bright, alpaca blanket
palms press tight this silky fur-made-cloth
while memory mocks my fist,
stealing in with once
the way your body let its guard go
arching back against the sink
in a silent house.
We pressed our passion,
aching toward desire and release
we could not know.
But still, that fierce kiss and fertile yearning
for a weak-kneed primal-chime
keeps me prayerful, leaning toward
a once and future final time.

I want to find you in silence,
warm and soft and smelling of sleep,
pajamas askew and mildly sweaty.
You are curled on your side,
flushed cheeks, heart racing, waiting
for me to complete the s of your body,
wrap you with mine.
My right hand circles you, rests against your rib cage,
pulls you close. I brush your breasts
with my arm, the length of me glued next to you.
We find a rhythm with our breathing,
I exhale against the back of your neck
and pray this silken fantasy
becomes a pas de deux.

This secret "we"
makes me smile
Fine times I store away
for lonely hours
when mind needs to conquer matter.
What's the matter with us?
A note passed in ninth grade,
text for your eyes only,
a joke remembered,
jest explained,
a treasured truth for two.
Truth be told,
I like our secret love
and the meeting of eyes
that shares unspoken souls'
desire. I hold it close,
this charm,
and arm myself against invaders.
A sweet dessert is ours
for all the unknown hours
to unfold.

In my fantasy world
I come to you at 3 a.m.
Soundless, I slide beneath the covers,
flimsy armor 'gainst a hostile world.
We are two halves made whole,
fit together lock and key.
Cocooned, no one can see
or hear or judge.
Phantom hands caress
our bodies while we,
pretending to sleep,
disown those fingers
seeking comfort, warmth,
hidden places, dark and soft
and damp.
No lamp lit to render truth,
we are outside the law,
pioneers in gumshoe justice,
private eyes
looking for clues to
life's unanswered questions,
listening to time
pinioned like a butterfly
if only in my mind.

The incipient "we" of "us"
pretends to find footing,
slips on new mown lawn,
unstable fable.
My autumn attitude
fields spring questions...
Where do we go from here?
The choice:
pick wild flowers in a fertile field
or rake dead leaves in the Fall?

Now I deal with doubts,
bogus benefits of love let loose
in my golden years.
I could be fonder of insects invading my brain
than this, this open sewer of fear,
mistrust and dull, dead null.
I was a fool to think that love could quicken
in my barely beating heart.

My soul sobs
shedding tears no one can see
Will we ever be free
to be?
I cry for your warmth
and soft body!
In my arms you belong.
Wrong, I know,
but, oh! my love,
the song you sing
draws me to the far shore
A shipwreck, yes,
but I will let the rocks rack
my shell, and free
this heart, too smart for rhyme.

The end of the rainbow
eludes my grasp
I can see it, but can't clasp
uneven edges of its arc.
Brilliant colors slip through my fingers
like so much tempera paint
in pre-school.
Swirling to muddy brown
it drips to the ground,
mirrors my impure desires,
and taints this love with lies.
I must keep these colors clear
and distinct, my dear,
like your aura
crystalline, pure
dazzling red and blue and green.
The hue of our love
will fade into night.
Without bright sun,
the rainbow's light is done.

The time ticks by
furthering distance and desire
alternating lust and despair,
with a twinge in the south land
set to titillate and fire
lustful thoughts. I must cloak these feelings.
Kill them. They do nothing to further
Happy Household Harmony.
What the hell. . .
My happiness doesn't matter,
don't you see?
In order to be happy,
I must be free.
And I'm not.

Women don't hit women
except when they do.
We could compare bruises,
mine physical,
yours mental,
if we spoke.
I, though, see you leaving me
each day in technicolor
red to purple to black to green to yellow.
There is no pain
just a mocking rainbow
fading
as my love has.

Alone
with the bruises
of a love gone wrong
no song to sing,
no words to say
the sorrow in my heart
heals slowly. . .
And I hope for you
a fresh start,
success
and joy.

Now I wonder
Did you plan
the final outrage,
hitting me with your left arm
while I drove
two handed,
waiting for the next blow?
I didn't mind
your punching
my shoulder.
Then, at least,
you weren't opening the car door,
threatening to jump out
at 70 mph.
Or christening me
with the bottle of water
I so thoughtfully provided
for the 60 miles we drove
to a destination unreached
and unreachable.
The anticipated leg of lamb
was not purchased that day,
while behind the wheel, the sacrificial lamb
dodged death by driving.

You will never see my feet,
cute as they are.
We will never sit in the sulphur smelling hot tub at Esalen
or hike the Pacific rim
or eat in the same restaurant at the same time.
You will avoid me as if I were a mosquito
carrying the Zika virus
and you a gravid girl pregnant with rage.
At my age, loss cultures night,
I am sorry. . . for what?
For loving you,
and that my pearl-like toes
will never kiss yours

Do you feel the pull,
after all this time?
Two months sail past,
and I,
I still drive by.
Can't shake like a dog
to rid myself of fleas.
No, my brain shouts "please"
and listens to the tinny echo of your voice.
If only you could seize me!
"Carpe Diem" to all your days
without "us."
We will never future be,
but I,
I see you still
in tactile memory

The storm brings you back to me.
Porch swing and violence of lightening,
thunder grips my body like
the force of your arms held firmly next my spine,
ears roaring, and blindness of a temporary sort
short circuit connections and leave me
still and spent and stunned.
Do you wonder why the sky
aimed arrows at our feet?
I, for one, want to die a death
determined by a random and capricious God,
theatrical, and flavored with a sense of humor, too,
while you, I think, would rather keep your options open,
ride a symphony into a frozen landscape,
future thaw a mundane miracle or two

Since I last saw you:
Dahlias bloomed on the right-of-way,
flowering riot of color and size.
A rescue kitty, sweet faced, prim,
flicked a wicked tail of displeasure,
purred her way into my heart.
Nine consecutive slot wins
at casinos we never knew together.
Democrats sad defeat.
Now I scour the weekly news
for mention of you,
try to read the lines
between which lie
desire, fear, despair.
But every milestone passes,
each weekend and holiday tally
and force our affair that never was
into a closed room crammed
with antique charm
bequeathed in deed to youth.
I hide
beneath an armed insurrection
of political correctness.
And still, you appear in my dreams,
and still, you are more real than the night.

ABOUT THE AUTHOR

Margo is a poet whose body of work has primarily remained buried in her desk drawer. After teaching for 40 years, her collection *Tangled Threads*, winner of the 2016 Blue Light Press Poetry Prize Competition, marks her entry into publishing. Margo shares her life with her partner of 23 years, two daughters, and a granddaughter in Fairfield, Iowa, a town of multiple marvels and 10,000 marvelous folk.